THE VIGELAND PARK
IN OSLO

By:
TONE WIKBORG
Former Chief Curator, Vigeland Museum

NORMANNS KUNSTFORLAG - OSLO
Photo: Urpo Tarnanen & Normanns Kunstforlag.
All works by Gustav Vigeland are reproduced with the
permission of the copyright holders via BONO.
© Vigeland Museum/BONO 2009

Gustav Vigeland

GUSTAV VIGELAND

Gustav Vigeland (1869-1943) was born in the south-coast town of Mandal in Norway. For centuries his ancestors had lived as farmers in a nearby valley, but his father became a master carpenter with his own furniture workshop. He was a devout follower of the Protestant Pietistic movement and the artist's childhood was spent in a strictly religious atmosphere.

Vigeland's artistic talents were first revealed in his drawing and woodcarving and at the age of fifteen his father took him to Oslo to apprentice him to a master. On the death of his father only two years later, Vigeland was compelled to return to Mandal and relinquish all hopes of becoming a sculptor. Helping his mother to support the family took most of his time, but every free moment was spent in reading and drawing. His favourite literature was Homer and the ancient Greek dramas, but he also read about and studied a great deal of anatomy and art, particularly the sculptures of the Danish neo-Classicist, Bertel Thorvaldsen.

In 1888 Vigeland was again back in the capital, this time taking with him a bundle of sketches for statues, groups and reliefs, their motifs mostly deriving from Greek mythology and the Bible. It proved impossible to earn a living as a woodcarver and after a period of severe hardship, he finally decided to contact the sculptor, Brynjulf Bergslien. Impressed by Vigeland's drawings, Bergslien took him into his studio and gave him his first practical training. Some months later, Vigeland was able to exhibit his first sculpture at the State Exhibition of Art in 1889. For a short period he attended the School of Design.

Vigeland's talent was soon recognized and he received several grants that enabled him to travel. He never attended an art academy but worked and studied on his own. He spent 1891 in Copenhagen where he was allowed to work on his own sculptures in the studio of V. Bissen. In 1893 he was in Paris where he remained for six months. The work of Auguste Rodin, seen by Vigeland on visits to the artist's studio, made a perceptible impact; inspiration from the Gates of Hell can be seen in Vigeland's relief "Hell", the magnum opus of his early years (1894-97, bronze in the National Gallery in Oslo, plaster in the Vigeland Museum). Rodin's intimate treatment of the relationship between man and woman was also influential in Vigeland's lifelong development of this theme.

A long-standing wish to visit Italy became a reality in 1895. On his way to Florence he spent a few months in Berlin, mixing there with an international Symbolist circle. Among these was the Polish author S. Prszybyszewski who wrote the first monograph on Gustav Vigeland, entitled «Auf den Wegen der Seele" ("The Path of the Soul"), in which he considers Vigeland an opponent of Realism in art. In Italy, to which he returned once again in 1896, he devoted himself to art studies of Antiquity and the Renaissance. "Every day I realise that sculpture must be stricter", he wrote home, revealing ideals of a more monumental sculpture, different from the modern Rodinesque style. Many years were to pass, however, before such ideals found an outlet in his own sculptures.

The grants came to an end and in order to make a living, Vigeland took on commissions for the restoration work of the mediaeval cathedral in Trondheim from 1897-1902. Among his works here are the sculptures for the choir and gargoyles for the towers. Inspired by fantasy sculptures from the Middle Ages, he took up the motif of Man in combat with dragons and lizards which, according to Christian tradition, are symbols of evil and hostile powers. This theme was to reappear in several later sculptures.

Around the turn of the century, Vigeland created many portraits of prominent Norwegians and received commissions for several memorials. His most remarkable creation as a sculptor, however, is the wealth of statuary in Vigeland Park.

The Municipality of Oslo was to show Vigeland exceptional generosity, ¬not only in connection with the park. In 1921 an agreement was drawn up in which Vigeland was to be provided with a new and spacious studio. In return, Vigeland would bequeath to the city all works of art in his possession as well as all original models of future sculptures. Vigeland lived and worked in the palatial building from 1924 until his death in 1943. In 1947 the studio was opened to the public as a museum for all his works. The present Vigeland Museum also serves as the mausoleum of the artist; the urn containing his ashes is placed in the building's tower.

VIGELAND PARK

Vigeland Park, which has partially become an integrated part of the older Frogner Park, covers an area of 80 acres. It functions both as a sculpture park and a public park, open to visitors day and night the whole year round.

The park contains 214 sculptures with more than 758 figures, all modelled in full size by Gustav Vigeland without the assistance of pupils or other artists. He also designed the architectural setting and the layout of the grounds with their expansive lawns and long, straight avenues bordered by maple trees.

Vigeland Park, however, was not originally conceived as the entity we see today. It is the result of a process stretching over a period of about 40 years, as part was added to part. The initial point was the Fountain. In 1900 Vigeland had made a small model of six men supporting a saucer-shaped vessel of water. He presented it to the City of Oslo, hoping it would be ordered for a minor square. Before receiving a negative response, he had already conceived the idea of a much larger fountain which he developed during the next years. In 1906 he presented his project to the public in the form of a 1/5 scale model; the six carrying

men had become giants and were placed in the centre of a large basin. Twenty groups of trees combined with human figures were placed on the surrounding parapet, the outer face of which was decorated with a continuous series of reliefs. The exhibition evoked great enthusiasm. A committee was formed to raise funds and to negotiate with the Municipality of Oslo. In 1907 it was decided that the fountain should be erected in front of Stortinget, the Norwegian Parliament.

With the sculptures nearly completed, Vigeland, in the meantime, had devised a plan for a series of granite groups to be added to the fountain. In 1916 he revealed his new plans and once again they won public acclaim; the Municipal Council supported him and wealthy admirers of his work made contributions. As the original site was too small for the new project, Vigeland's proposal to place the fountain in the Palace grounds was accepted. It was to be reached from Karl Johan's street by semi-circular stairs on which he planned to place the granite groups. This new project also included a number of groups of humans and lizards in combat; four of these can be seen today in Vigeland Park, on tall columns at each corner of the Bridge.

When Vigeland was promised a new studio at Frogner in 1921, he changed his plans again and proposed placing the fountain, the granite groups and the latest addition, the Monolith - a column of human figures to be carved in granite - on the site immediately outside. The Municipal Council was not satisfied with this solution and in 1922 asked Vigeland to prepare a plan for placing the sculptures in connection with Frogner Park. Vigeland responded promptly and presented a new plan. It met with considerable opposition and only in 1924, after two years of heated debate, was it approved.

Further additions were to follow. In 1928, Vigeland's plan for the park's main entrance fronting on Kirkeveien was accepted. In 1931 followed a renewal of the bridge over the Frogner ponds, with the addition of numerous sculptures on the parapets. The grounds to the west of the ponds were also extended considerably. For the rest of his life Vigeland continued to model new sculptures for the park and in 1947 the Municipal Council adopted the plans as they existed at the time of Vigeland's death. The numerous works are primarily grouped in five units along a main axis extending from the monumental entrance facing Kirkeveien in the east to the Wheel of Life in the west. These units will not be described in chronological order, but rather as they meet the eye of the visitor walking through the Main Entrance.

MAIN ENTRANCE

The Main Entrance consists of five large gates and two smaller pedestrian gates in wrought iron. Railings curve outwards on each side and are terminated by two small gatehouses. The final designs for the wrought-iron gates were made in 1926 and exhibited in 1927 together with some details executed in iron. The upper

parts, surmounted by lanterns, show a marked change of style; they were designed in the 1930's to replace the original ones. A large donation from a Norwegian bank facilitated the forging of the gates and for this purpose Vigeland set up a smithy outside his studio and employed highly skilled workers.

The five large gates consist of two doors, each with three circular panels within quadratic frames. The top and bottom panels have ornaments of abstracted twigs and branches in a geometric pattern, a different design in each gate. Three-dimensional lizards fill the central panel in each, demonstrating the remarkable skill of the smiths. In the middle gate, lizards are intertwined with intricate wrought-iron ropework.

The panels in the other gates depict lizards in wild combat, a motif possibly inspired by the dragon reliefs in wood at the entrances of Norwegian mediaeval stave churches. The copper-roofed Gate Houses are topped by gilt Weather Vanes in the shape of horizontal figures, a man and a woman. The doors are of bronze, each with six small reliefs (1942). The basic shape of each relief is a circle formed by human figures and lizards, a theme first adopted by Vigeland while executing sculptures for the restoration of the mediaeval cathedral in Trondheim. The meaning of the animal imagery is ambiguous. It may symbolise hostile or evil forces that accompany Man throughout life. Even what appears to be a foetus is completely entangled in the animal.

THE BRIDGE

From the entrance gates, paths skirt either side of a spacious lawn leading to the Bridge which is 328 ft long and 49 ft wide. On the granite parapets stand 58 single figures or groups in bronze (1926-33). Each of the four corners of the Bridge is flanked by a granite group, each set on a tall column in the same material. Three of these depict a man struggling with a giant lizard, while the fourth shows a woman submitting to the embrace of a lizard. Models for these groups date back to 1916-17, when Vigeland was planning a whole series of such sculptures in connection with the fountain project.

The sculptures on the Bridge portray people of widely differing ages, although there is less emphasis on old age than in the next two units in the park. Many characteristic representations of children are noticeable. Dominant motifs among the groups are the relationships between man and woman and between adults and children. The representation of mother and child has a long and popular tradition in art. A more unusual theme is the father and child relationship, which is the subject of several sculptures.

At the point where the Bridge widens, one finds at each side, a circular sculpture with a more pronounced symbolic motif. One of the bronze wheels encloses a man and a woman linked together in a rotating movement. The circle being a well-known symbol of eternity, the sculpture may indicate the constant attraction and love between the sexes or a figurative version of the Eastern symbol of

"Yin and Yang". In the sculpture opposite, a man fights to break out of the imprisoning ring. Figures in repose alternate with dynamic figures in energetic or violent motion. The vitality and zest for life emanating from these sculptures are otherwise not so frequently found in Vigeland's art. All the figures face either onto the Bridge or parallel to it. The contours are firm and simple, the forms broad and rounded. The surface is covered by tiny "pats" to attain an even distribution of light.

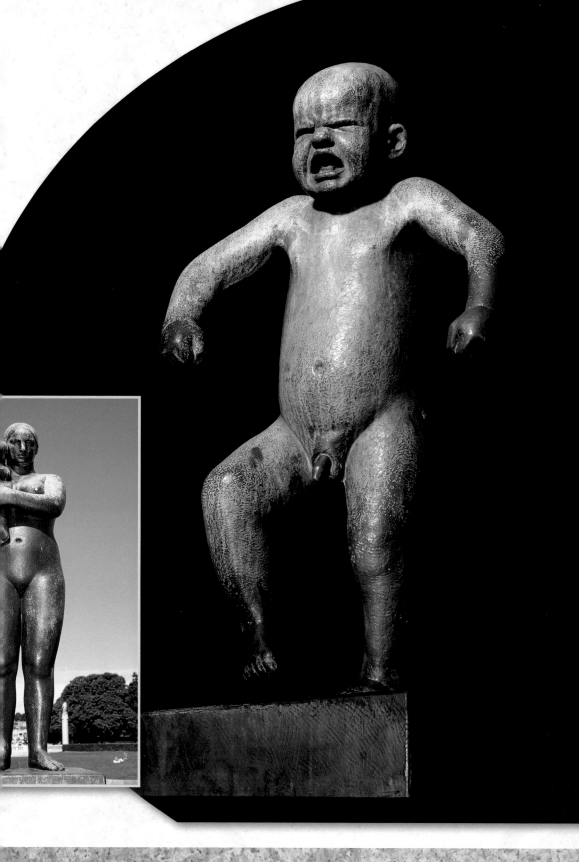

THE CHILDREN'S PLAYGROUND

Just below the bridge is a circular area with eight bronze sculptures of small children placed around its circumference (1940). In the centre, mounted on a small granite column is the figure of an unborn child, head down (1923). The children surrounding it depict the very earliest stage of life.

THE FOUNTAIN

Beyond the Bridge, the path continues through a rose garden to the Fountain, the earliest sculpture unit in the park. In the centre of the basin six giants hold the large saucer-shaped vessel aloft and from it a curtain of water spills down around them. The men, representing different ages, may be interpreted as toiling with the burden of life and the effort expended in lifting the heavy vessel varies. Water, a universal symbol of fertility, is used within the fountain complex in a meaningful juxtaposition with the twenty tree groups on the surrounding parapet, the latter evidently symbolising "the tree of life". There is, furthermore, a formal resemblance as the trees repeat on a smaller scale the silhouette of the central group; a wide compact top with a pierced, gradually tapered base.

The combination of human beings and trees in 6.5-feet-high sculptures is one of Vigeland's most original concepts. The tree crowns and branches create a sculptural space that lends itself admirably to the multitude of positions for the figures and light and shadow vary according to the weather and changing hours of the day. Although the trees have a similar outline, they are all formed differently. Some even assume fantasy shapes, such as a long-necked animal in No. 11, or even a living organism tying an unhappy, falling couple together in No. 13.

The tree groups represent a romantic expression of Man's relationship to nature. They also form the setting for life's evolving stages, stretching from childhood and adolescence through adulthood to old age and death. Each stage is depicted in groups of five which are placed together at the four corners of the basin. This cycle of life starts towards the north with a swarm of tiny children amidst the branches. Vigeland would call them "geniuses", symbols of the inherent fertility of life. In the next group a boy is sitting in the tree, followed by boys actively climbing the tree while girls stand quietly around the trunk. A young girl gliding through the branches, wide-eyed and with hands pressed against her breasts, may be seen as representing puberty. The next section begins with a young woman dreamily leaning outwards from the tree and ends with a young man, lost in thought, standing within the tree space. Between them are three groups depicting different love scenes.

In the third corner, life has become more complicated. A woman in a melancholy attitude is sitting on a tree which is shaped like an animal. Next to her a small child is placed alone in the tree and on its other side a couple plummets downward through the tree. A man with an anguished expression climbs and coils himself around a tree, followed by an angry man trying to drive away babies in a tree-top. In the fourth corner old people are effectively grouped together with children, the new generation that will continue the course of life. Finally, death in the shape of a skeleton has taken its place among the branches.

The themes of the different stages of life, and life as part of an eternal cycle are repeated in the frieze of sixty bronze reliefs on the parapet beneath. They also introduce the relationship of Man to animals; children play happily with them, women are affectionate and trustful while a man is seen fighting a wolf. The transition from death to new life is shown in the form of skeletons sinking down and disintegrating. Tiny geniuses collect the remains and fly away with them. The swarm of geniuses -, symbols of

fertility - now take over the empty reliefs. The cycle is complete; out of death new life arises.

The reliefs are always rendered on a plain background. The use of the relief area varies considerably. It may be covered by a few figures or be almost empty, as when a single figure lies outstretched at the bottom. Changes in form and style can be discerned in the tree groups and particularly in the reliefs. In the earliest figures the modelling is analytic, with a detailed naturalism which develops into a broader and more rounded form (for comparison see tree groups No. 7 and No. 6, modelled in 1907 and 1912 respectively).

THE LABYRINTH

The ground around the Fountain is paved with mosaics in black and white granite. Its pattern forms a labyrinth with a 'path' extending a distance of nearly 3000 metres or nearly 2 miles. The design consists of 16 circles enclosed by square frames all linked together. Every circle has the same basic pattern but the details are all different.

There is no centre as the Fountain is placed there, and unlike most labyrinths it has a separate entrance and exit. The Labyrinth is a meaningful adjunct to the sculptural world of the Fountain; it may be interpreted as an image of the journey through life with its twists and blind alleys until, with great patience, the way out is found at last.

THE MONOLITH PLATEAU

From the Fountain the path continues upwards to the highest point in the sculpture park. The Monolith plateau (394 x 197 feet) is reached by ascending three terraces. Eight entrances give access to the plateau through Figural Gates in wrought iron. These were designed by Vigeland in the 1930's and executed in his own smithy. The gates represent an innovation in Vigeland's wrought iron work. The iron bars convey the outline of the human form as well as muscles, ribs, sinews and hair. Figures of various ages are both realistic and ornamental. In this purely two-dimensional art, Vigeland has also introduced movement and action in depth as in No. 5 in which three women walk along surrounded by decorative vines.

In the centre of the plateau circular stairs rise towards the Monolith. Placed on these in radiating rows are 36 groups in granite. As in the Fountain, the principal theme is the cycle of life. At the topmost stair level facing the Fountain is a compact group of children (geniuses, No. 1). In the equivalent position in the adjacent row, completing the circle when followed clockwise, is a group of lifeless bodies (No. 34). These two groups mark the beginning and end of the life cycle in which Man is depicted in a variety of typical human situations and relationships. A man and woman sit facing one another with a little child between them, the very image of "the family". Children play, young men and women dream and embrace. Old age is represented in several groups. The scenes are not without conflict and aggression; as shown for instance in group No. 24 where a man angrily throws aside a woman or in No. 14 where two boys tease a feeble-minded and helpless old man. Every sculpture includes at least two figures and human relationships are more emphasised than in the other sculptural units in the park. None of the groups exceeds 6.5 ft in height, but as the figures are over life-size only some of the children stand upright and the adults all sit or kneel, firmly anchored to the plinth. Their huge and solid forms convey the impression of an earthbound human race.

The groups show a certain variation in composition and form. Initially Vigeland wanted to retain the volume of the granite block with the result that the figures from this early period are particularly broad and simple with a minimum of surface detail. It was not long, however, before a greater differentiation in both composition and figure style was introduced and more space was allowed between the figures. Although a skilled carver himself, Vigeland did not sculpt directly in granite. He modelled the groups in full size and employed professional artisans to do the time-consuming work of transferring the original models into stone.

THE MONOLITH

The column which consists of 121 figures was modelled by Vigeland in the years 1924-25. It has been named the Monolith because it was carved out of a single block of stone. The figural part is 46.3 ft high and the total height, including the plinth, is 56.7 ft. The stone was quarried from a mountain at Iddefjorden on the south-east coast of Norway and in its final shape weighs c. 180 tons. It was carved at the present site where a shed was built to cover the stone and the full-size plaster model. Three stone carvers worked on the column daily from 1929 to 1943. The Monolith was finished just before Vigeland died.

The column is completely covered by human figures in relief, singly or in groups. At the bottom there are seemingly inert bodies. Above them, figures ascend in a spiral, the movement halting midway and then rising at a faster pace towards the summit which is covered by small children. Vigeland himself has compared the movement of the figures to a wave which rises, curves and finally ebbs away. While many of the figures seem to drift more or less unconsciously upwards, others are more active; some struggle not to fall, others lift and support each other.

Various interpretations of the Monolith have been suggested: a phallic symbol, the struggle for existence, Man's yearning for the spiritual spheres, transcendence of everyday life and cyclical repetition. Yet another interpretation is Man's resurrection. In support of this theory is the apparent link between the column figures and those in a large, unfinished relief from 1900, filled with ascending figures which Vigeland entitled "The Resurrection" (Vigeland Museum).

Vigeland himself wished to leave the question open. One of his few recorded comments on the subject is: "The granite groups depict life; the column belongs to the world of fantasy. The granite groups are easy to understand; the Monolith may be interpreted in many ways."

Leading down the western side of the Monolith plateau is a series of terraces. A few steps further on is a Sundial, mounted on a 12-sided granite pedestal bearing circular reliefs depicting the signs of the Zodiac (1930).

The final sculpture along the main axial path is the Wheel of Life (1933-34). Four adult figures and three children are linked together in a circular composition around a void. The sculpture measures 9.8 ft in diameter. Mounted on a plinth with a low pyramidal top, the group appears to be rotating. The cycle-of-life concept, the connecting theme in the fountain sculptures and the granite groups, is here compressed into one single sculpture and the Wheel of Life further emphasises the interdependence of human beings.

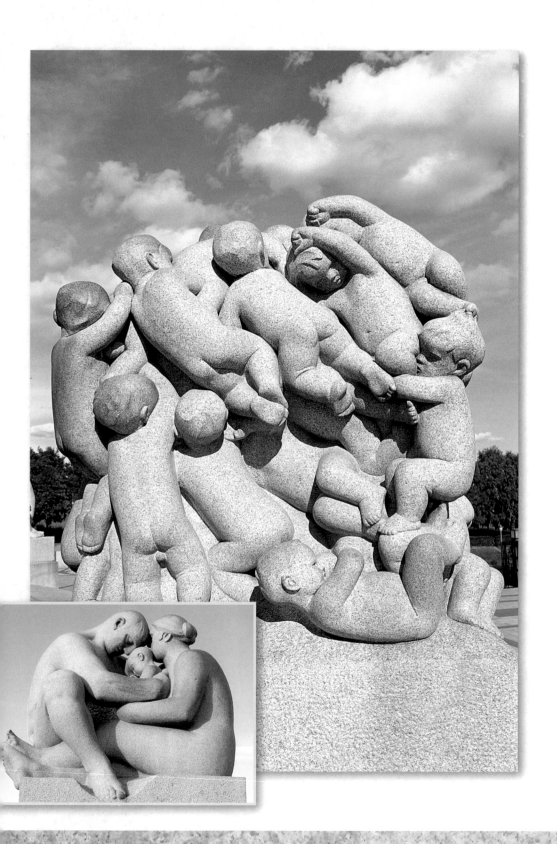

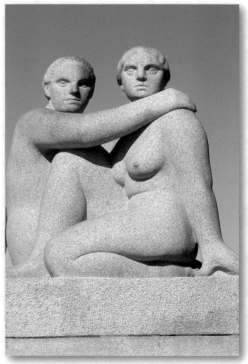

SCULPTURES OUTSIDE THE MAIN AXIS

A second axis intersects the main axis at the Fountain. Its northern end is marked by low, triangular terraces surmounted by a group in bronze, the Clan, placed on a 13 ft tall pediment (1934-36). With the exception of the Monolith, this group is Vigeland's largest sculpture and consists of 21 figures. Due to lack of funds the group remained stored in plaster in the Vigeland Museum until 1985 when a gift from IBM made it possible to have it cast in bronze and erected in the park in 1988, according to Vigeland's original plan.

The figures are disposed in minor groups, all repeating the motif of protection: a mother shields her children, older children take care of the smaller ones, the old ones huddle together. Two men stand, one at each end as if to guard them all from a menacing threat. Vigeland's intention was evidently to portray one of Man's deepest instincts, the protection of kin.

Sculptures outside the second terrace between the Fountain and the Monolith plateau include, at the north end, the Young girl kneeling, encircled by a coiled lizard (1938) and at the south end by the group, Young boy and girl leaning against each other over a well (1939).

Near the Vigeland Museum to the south, the bronze group Triangle (1938) is placed on a circular extension in the diagonal path leading from the Monolith: Two heavy women plunge down from each side and clutch an elderly, stocky man. To the north inside the Main Entrance stands Vigeland's self-portrait (1942). Dressed in his everyday working clothes, with hammer and chisel in hand, he stands as a signature of his own work. Opposite this statue, a large granite stone has been erected containing the names of those who have contributed to the realisation of the sculptures and the park, both in Vigeland's time and later.

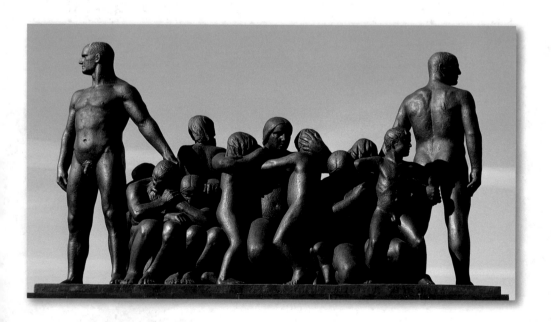

THE VIGELAND MUSEUM is about five minutes' walk from the Sculpture Park. It was built by the Municipality of Oslo as a studio and residence for Gustav Vigeland, and in return the sculptor donated nearly all his works to the city - a transaction unparalleled in the history of art. Vigeland moved into the new building, which covers almost an acre, in 1924, living in apartments on the top floor of the East Wing. Here he resided and worked until his death in 1943. The Museum, which houses some 1,600 sculptures, 12,000 drawings and 420 woodcuts, was opened in 1947. On display are the works of Vigeland's early years, his portraits and monuments and several hundred plastic sketches. The visitor can trace his development as an artist and acquire an illuminating insight into the work of his fertile mind and artistic talent.

Henrik Ibsen.
Plaster. 1903

Mother and child.
Marble. 1909

Young man and woman.
Marble. 1906

THE BRIDGE. PLAN OF THE SCULPTURES.

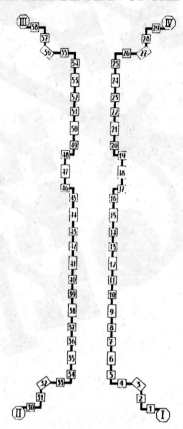

The corners of the Bridge: Lizard groups in granite.

I.   Lizard embracing a woman. 1918.
II.   Man fighting small lizard. Ca. 1930.
III. Man fighting lizard. 1918.
IV.   Lizard clutching naked man. 1930.

The parapets of the Bridge: 58 figures and groups in bronze. 1926-1933.

1. Boy with baby on his head.
2. Man carrying two babies.
3. Man swinging boy.
4. Woman with baby on her arm.
5. Two girls behind each other.
6. Man running with a boy on his back.
7. Girl facing woman.
8. Girl with her hands on her head.
9. Man lifting girl.
10. Young man, hands behind his back.
11. Man with arms crossed on his chest.
12. Old man hitting boy.
13. Woman, hands in front of mouth.
14. Elderly man and young man.
15. Man lifting woman in front of him.
16. Woman standing behind man.
17. Little girl, laughing.
18. Man and woman inside a ring.
19. Little boy looking to the side.
20. Man standing behind woman.
21. Man carrying woman in front of him.
22. Young woman with clenched fists.
23. Young woman, head bent to the left.
24. Young woman, dancing.
25. Man, hands fixed behind his neck.
26. Man carrying boy around his neck.
27. Man playing with four children (geniuses).
28. Old man walking with little boy.
29. Man with both hands on his chest.
30. Girl with baby on her head.
31. Woman with baby in her arms.
32. Woman lifting baby in front of her.
33. Little girl standing behind woman.
34. Two boys looking up.
35. Woman carrying sleeping child.
36. Girl standing in front of woman.
37. Young woman, hands on her hips.
38. Two boys running.
39. Man with hands on his hips.
40. Young man with arms at his sides.
41. Man and woman dancing.
42. Woman with hands behind her back.
43. Woman with arms at her sides.
44. Man tilting woman over his head.
45. Man and woman against each other.
46. Angry little boy, crying.
47. Man inside a ring.
48. Little girl, arms stretched out.
49. Man standing behind woman.
50. Man running.
51. Woman with arms above her head.
52. Woman, laughing.
53. Woman jumping up on a man.
54. Man with baby in his arms.
55. Boy standing in front of man.
56. Man lifting elderly man.
57. Old man with boy on his back.
58. Man looking to the right.

THE FOUNTAIN. PLAN OF THE SCULPTURES.

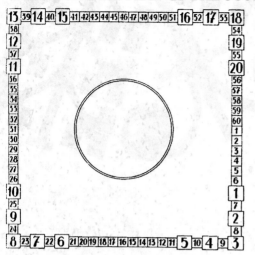

Tree groups. Bronze. 1906-1914.
1. Swarm of 18 babies (geniuses).
2. Boy sitting in a tree, listening.
3. Two boys climbing.
4. Three little girls standing around a tree.
5. Girl gliding down between the branches.
6. Young woman leaning out of the tree.
7. Young boy and girl, standing forehead to forehead.
8. Man standing behind woman.
9. Man embracing woman.
10. Man standing under the tree: "The dreamer".
11. Woman sitting on animal-like tree.
12. Baby sitting in tree.
13. Man and woman plunging downwards, entwined by branches.
14. Man climbing the tree, his body horizontal.
15. Angry man chasing children.
16. Man clinging to the tree.
17. Old woman and small boy.
18. Old man and boy.
19. Old man sitting, clinging to tree.
20. Skeleton sitting in tree.

Reliefs. Bronze. 1906-1936.
1. Small boy (genius) on a prehistoric animal.
2. Five children (geniuses) collecting bones.
3. Eight children (geniuses) gliding through the air.
4. Foal kicking little boy.
5. Foal and two children (geniuses).
6. Four children (geniuses) playing with a wolf.
7. Five children and bear-cub.
8. Four boys in a row, holding each other's hands.
9. Two girls tending Lambs.
10. Boy turning towards crying baby.
11. Two girls carrying babies.
12. Three boys fighting.
13. Three boys standing in a group.
14. Three dancing girls.
15. Two girls playing with babies.
16. Boy fighting an eagle.
17. Girls with fighting babies.
18. Two girls playing.
19. Boy grasping a girl by the neck.
20. Two girls lifting a dwarf.
21. Dwarf lifting young woman.
22. Young man recumbent.
23. Boy holding girl by the shoulders.
24. Boy and girl facing each other.
25. Recumbent woman.
26. Boy and girl standing back to back.
27. Young man with closed eyes, head surrounded by four geniuses. "The dreamer".
28. Old woman chasing girl.
29. Two young women at play.
30. Woman sitting in the horns of a reindeer.
31. Woman and baby lying on sea-bed, fish swimming towards them.
32. Young woman riding a bear.
33. Recumbent boy, a woman glides above him. "The dream".
34. Two young women gliding in the air.
35. Elderly woman facing young woman.
36. Woman and unicorn.
37. Recumbent baby.
38. Woman standing between two men.
39. Man standing between woman and young girl.
40. Man and woman dancing.
41. Woman kneeling behind seated man. "Consolation".
42. Mother, father and child.
43. Woman between man and child.
44. Man and woman with dead child.
45. Man and woman floating in the air.
46. Old man kicking wolf
47. Fat man and frightened girl.
48. Old man and two boys.
49. Two seated men.
50. Old man crawling on the ground. "The hermit".
51. Old man and woman.
52. Old man lying on his back.
53. Old woman leading two small children by the hands.
54. Old woman blessing small boy.
55. Old woman lying dead.
56. Death (skeleton) separating man and woman.
57. Three falling men.
58. Five sinking skeletons.
59. Male and female skeletons.
60. Disintegrating skeletons.

36 GRANITE GROUPS. 1915-1936.

1. Swarm of babies (geniuses).
2. Man and woman sitting with baby between them.
3. Woman stooping towards numerous children.
4. Group of children.
5. Old man embracing four boys.
6. Boy and girl riding on woman's back.
7. Group of eight little girls.
8. Two girls standing on their heads, smiling.
9. Four girls kneeling behind each other.
10. Man putting his hand on the shoulder of a boy who looks away.
11. Three girls lifting a boy.
12. Boys fighting.
13. Two young men sitting beside each other.
14. Two boys teasing an imbecile man.
15. Three boys kneeling, "watching a bird".
16. Young man and woman, sitting back to back.
17. Young boy and girl. "Taken by surprise".
18. Young man bending down towards young woman.
19. Woman crouching behind man's back.
20. Old woman laying her hand on the head of young woman. "The blessing".
21. Old woman dressing the hair of a young woman.
22. Sitting man and woman, their foreheads touching.
23. Young man and woman sitting apart.
24. Man throwing woman.
25. Two young women.
26. Elderly man and smiling young woman.
27. Man kneeling behind woman, embracing her.
28. Two men sitting back to back.
29. Two men fighting.
30. Old woman laying her hand on the shoulder of young man, who is looking away.
31. Two old men.
32. Old woman resting against old man.
33. Two old women behind each other, listening.
34. Pile of lifeless bodies.
35. Three old-women sitting beside each other.
36. Standing man lifting dead man.